MW01596487

HARRY'S HOUSE
By Harry Styles • 2022

MUSIC FOR A SUSHI RESTAURANT

LATE NIGHT TALKING

GRAPEJUICE

AS IT WAS

DAYLIGHT

LITTLE FREAK

MATILDA

CINEMA

DAYDREAMING

KEEP DRIVING

SATELLITE

BOYFRIENDS

LOVE OF MY LIFE

MUSIC FOR A
SUSHI RESTAURANT

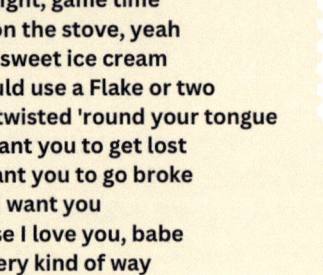

Green eyes, fried rice
I could cook an egg on you
Late night, game time
Coffee on the stove, yeah
You're sweet ice cream
But you could use a Flake or two
Blue bubblegum twisted 'round your tongue
I don't want you to get lost
I don't want you to go broke
I want you
It's 'cause I love you, babe
In every kind of way
Just a little taste
Know I love you, babe
(You know I love you, babe)
Excuse me, green tea
Music for a sushi restaurant
From ice on rice
Scuba-duba-do-boo-boo
Music for a sushi restaurant
Music for a sushi restaurant
Music for whatever you want
Scuba-duba-do-boo-boo
I'm not going to get lost
I'm not going to go broke
Staying cool
(Know I love you, babe)
(You know I love you, babe)
If the stars were edible
And our hearts were never full
Could we live with just a taste?
Just a taste
It's 'cause I love you, babe
In every kind of way
Just a little taste
Know I love you, babe
(You know I love you, babe)

MUSIC FOR A SUSHI RESTAURANT

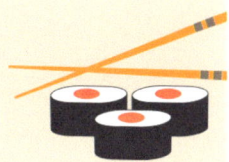

The album's (Harry's House) opening song, "Music for a Sushi Restaurant," is a real attention-grabber, and it was actually in the running to be the album's name. Harry recalled to NPR being in a sushi restaurant in LA with his producer. "I kind of said, like, 'This is really strange music for a sushi restaurant,' and then I was like, 'Oh, that would be a really fun album title'". On it's face, the song seems a little silly and fun, but basically it's "about ingredients for making sushi while relating it to his desire for a relationship," according to Genius. I mean, how much money would you pay for Harry to imply that you're so hot that he can, indeed, "cook an egg on you"? The only answer here is your entire life savings. Using food as a metaphor is pretty on brand for Harry too, since we know "Watermelon Sugar" has not a damn thing to do with watermelons.

However, the music video reveals a very different attitude with Styles acting as a fairytale siren in a restaurant kitchen. This ingenious video is a huge metaphor for the hot and cold, toxic and vapid nature and culture for the music industry. It also beautifully demonstrates the objectification of artists in the music industry, as well as them becoming products and commodities – rather than people.

Once Styles' voice is no longer good enough, or he makes a single mistake, he is literally killed by the kitchen staff – showing viewers the brutality and intense pressure many artists or musicians must be under to live up to high standards and to constantly keep up appearances. This is also a brilliant way to represent how quick and feeble the industry is – constantly searching for the next best, shiny and new product to carry on creating profit for the bigger players in the company.

LATE NIGHT TALKING

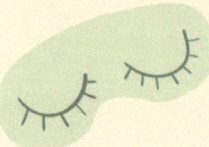

Things haven't been quite the same
There's a haze on the horizon, babe
It's only been a couple of days
And I miss you, mm, yeah
When nothin' really goes to plan
You stub your toe or break your camera
I'll do everythin' I can
To help you through
If you're feelin' down
I just wanna make you happier, baby
Wish I was around
I just wanna make you happier, baby
We've been doin' all this late night talkin'
'Bout anythin' you want until the mornin'
Now you're in my life
I can't get you off my mind
I've never been a fan of change
But I'd follow you to any place
If it's Hollywood or Bishopsgate
I'm coming too
If you're feelin' down
I just wanna make you happier, baby
Wish I was around
I just wanna make you happier, baby
We've been doin' all this late night talkin'
'Bout anythin' you want until the mornin'
Now you're in my life
I can't get you off my mind
Can't get you off my mind
Can't get you off my mind (can't get you off my mind)
I won't even try (I won't even try)
To get you off my mind (get you off my mind)
We've been doin' all this late night talkin'
'Bout anythin' you want until the mornin'
Now you're in my life
I can't get you off my mind
Can't get you off my mind (all this late night talkin')
Can't get you off my mind (all this late night talkin')
I won't even try (all this late night talkin')
Can't get you off my
All this late night talkin'

LATE NIGHT TALKING

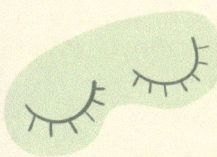

"Late Night Talking" is the second track on Harry Styles' 2022 album 'Harry's House.' In the song, Harry reminisces all the late-night talks of sweet nothings he has had with a former partner. It only takes twenty-one days to form a habit, and all their late-night talks have made Harry an addict to a special euphoria.

When the song first debuted, many fans believed that it was about Harry's now ex-girlfriend, Olivia Wilde, due to the mention of a "camera" in the first verse (she's a director BTW) and the reference to "Hollywood and Bishopsgate" in the second verse. Perhaps that line is a callout to their respective neighborhoods? Plus, it's apparent he's singing about a special someone when he sings in the third line, "It's only been a couple of days and I miss you."
But due to the fact that we see multiple love interests in the video, the song could be about his past relationships, or his take on sex and intimacy. Back in April, ahead of the Harry's House release, the artist opened up about his experience with dating, labels and sexuality.

The song appears to be addressing change in the general sense within a relationship, but also using that to talk about change within the industry. The first line "Things haven't been quite the same" has clear parallels to 'As It Was' showing that the theme of change is common throughout the album. Although this change seems exciting, it also brings about a sense of uncertainty: "There's a haze along the horizon babe" implies that the future of his relationship/industry is no longer clear. Towards the end of the song, Harry expresses that he can't physically be there for this person so instead they talk all night on the phone. The song is about being there for your person at whatever capacity you can and being hopeful in periods of change.

GRAPEJUICE

Yesterday, it finally came, a sunny afternoon
I was on my way to buy some flowers for you (ooh)
Thought that we could hide away in a corner of the heath
There's never been someone who's so perfect for me
But I got over it and I said
"Give me somethin' old and red"
I pay for it more than I did back then
There's just no gettin' through
Without you
A bottle of rouge
Just me and you
Sittin' in the garden, I'm a couple glasses in
I was tryna count up all the places we've been
You're always there, so don't overthink
I'm so over whites and pinks
I pay for it more than I did back then
There's just no gettin' through
Without you
A bottle of rouge
Just me and you
1982
Just me and you
There's just no gettin' through
The grape juice blues

GRAPEJUICE

The song "Grapejuice" by Harry Styles is an ode to a romantic relationship. In the song, Styles reflects fondly on a past adventure shared with his partner and contrasts it with the present moment. He longs to have that same sense of connection and nostalgia in their relationship, so he opts to buy a bottle of red wine, a classic French symbol of romance, so that they can experience it together. The title, as used in the chorus, actually points to letting go of "the grape juice blues". Said "grace juice", all lyrics considered, would actually be a reference to the wine.

Ultimately the song celebrates the beauty and power of enduring love. We already know that when Harry Styles gets to referring to fruits and the such, said song is likely going to rather be about romance. Every musician finds their muse in different places but we have to agree that fruits are vital part of Harry's source of inspiration for his music. And so it is with "Grapejuice".

It could be argued"Grapejuice" doesn't necessarily tell a sweet romantic story. It could also be hinting at his need for escapism with a stimulant such as red wine. He does mention that he was going to buy flowers for his partner, but instead, he went for a bottle of wine. This draws a clear line between emotional stimulants versus physical stimulants–and sacrifice versus self-fulfillment.

AS IT WAS

Holdin' me back
Gravity's holdin' me back
I want you to hold out the palm of your hand
Why don't we leave it at that?
Nothin' to say
When everything gets in the way
Seems you cannot be replaced
And I'm the one who will stay, oh

In this world, it's just us
You know it's not the same as it was
In this world, it's just us
You know it's not the same as it was
As it was, as it was
You know it's not the same
Answer the phone

"Harry, you're no good alone
Why are you sittin' at home on the floor?
What kind of pills are you on?"
Ringin' the bell
And nobody's comin' to help
Your daddy lives by himself
He just wants to know that you're well, oh

In this world, it's just us
You know it's not the same as it was
In this world, it's just us
You know it's not the same as it was
As it was, as it was
You know it's not the same
Go home, get ahead, light-speed internet
I don't wanna talk about the way that it was
Leave America, two kids follow her
I don't wanna talk about who's doin' it first
As it was
You know it's not the same as it was
As it was, as it was

AS IT WAS

The first impression the listener gets from Harry Styles' song, "As It Was," is a sample from Styles' goddaughter saying "Come on Harry, we want to say goodnight to you." It puts a warm feeling in your heart as you are invited into Harry's House.

Styles wrote the song during the COVID-19 pandemic, when there were extensive, worldwide lockdowns. It was a time of loneliness and isolation for many people, including celebrities. Saying that the world isn't the same "as it was" before a global pandemic might be the understatement of the century. But the observation also tied into his reflections on his life as an actor and a singer and how much it has changed since before he was discovered. In one interview, he said that the pandemic slowed life down, forcing him to reflect on himself not just as a musician, but as a friend, partner, and family member.

One line in As It Was seems to reference his former relationship with Olivia Wilde specifically: "Leave America, two kids follow her." She has two children from her previous relationship, Otis and Daisy. The children reportedly had a good relationship with Styles. Meanwhile, Styles and Wilde supposedly moved in together in London, initially coming from Los Angeles. They have both made public comments in the past about the difficulty of having a relationship between two extremely busy, high-profile figures, whose schedules often conflict and take them to opposite sides of the globe. With all these factors in mind, it seems like 'As It Was' certainly incorporates Styles' experiences with being in a long-distance relationship.

DAYLIGHT

I I'm on the roof, you're in your airplane seat
I was nose-bleeding, looking for life out there
Reading your horoscope, you were just doing cocaine
In my kitchen, you never listen, I hope you're missing me by now
If I was a bluebird, I would fly to you
You'd be the spoon
Dip you in honey so I could be sticking to you
Daylight, you got me cursing the daylight (ooh)
Daylight, you got me cursing the daylight (ooh)
Daylight, you got me calling at all times (ooh)
Ain't gonna sleep 'til the daylight (ooh)
Out of New York, I'm on the comedown speed
We're on bicycles, saying, "There's life out there"
You got the antidote, I'll take one to go, go, please
Get the picture, cut out my middle
You ain't got time for me right now
If I was a bluebird, I would fly to you
You'd be the spoon
Dip you in honey so I could be sticking to you
Ooh
Ooh
Daylight, you got me calling at all times (ooh)
Ain't gonna sleep 'til the daylight (ooh)
Daylight, you got me cursing the daylight (ooh)
Daylight, you got me cursing the daylight (ooh)
Daylight, you got me calling at all times (ooh)
Ain't gonna sleep 'til the daylight (ooh)
If I was a bluebird, I would fly to you
You'd be the spoon
Dip you in honey so I could be sticking to you

DAYLIGHT

"Daylight" by Harry Styles has sparked rumors about connections to his ex-girlfriend Taylor Swift who also has a song by the same name from her 2019 album 'Lover.' It is interesting to note how in Harry's song, Daylight is viewed as a negative thing, whereas Taylor views it as a positive. However, to shut down this speculation, during an interview with Howard Stern, Harry Styles denied any link saying "You are reading too much into it. You know I'd love to tell you that you're spot-on, but you're not. We will always wonder."

An alternative interpretation is that he is singing about being in a long-distance relationship, and he struggles to cope with the time difference between him and his partner. The song starts in the clearly familiar position of them being in two different places ie. "I'm on the roof, you're in your airplane seat." The distance between them means he is now having to guess and hope how they are feeling, to the point of reading their horoscope to try and guess what's going on in their life. He sings about how he wishes it were different and makes reference to the clearly inadequate coping mechanisms he relies on to fill the vacuum. Unfortunately, a lot of wishes are beyond us and he is forced to deal with the fact that they share a different daylight.

Furthermore, Styles could be dreaming about the person, which is why he's "cursing the daylight". When he's dreaming, he has access to this person. It could be interpreted in multiple ways but ultimately it is about separation, either physically or emotionally.

LITTLE FREAK

Little freak, Jezebel
You sit high atop the kitchen counter
Stay green a little while
You bring blue lights to dreams
Starry haze, crystal ball
Somehow, you've become some paranoia
A wet dream just dangling
But your gift is wasted on me
I was thinkin' about who you are
Your delicate point of view, I
Was thinkin' about you
I'm not worried about where you are
Or who you will go home to, I'm
Just thinkin' about you
Just thinkin' about you
Did you dress up for Halloween?
I spilt beer on your friend, I'm not sorry
A golf swing and a trampoline
Maybe we'll do this again
Tracksuit and a ponytail
You hide the body all that yoga gave you
Red wine and a ginger ale
But you would make fun of me, for sure
I was thinkin' about who you are
Your delicate point of view, I
Was thinkin' about you
I'm not worried about where you are
Or who you will go home to, I'm
Just thinkin' about you
I disrespected you
Jumped in feet first, and I landed too hard
A broken ankle, karma rules
You never saw my birthmark
I was thinkin' about who you are
Your delicate point of view, I
Was thinkin' about you
I'm not worried about where you are
Or who you will go home to, I'm
Just thinkin' about you
Just thinkin' about you
Just thinkin' about you

LITTLE FREAK

'Little Freak' isn't exactly what it appears to be from the title...it's actually quite a poignant and emotionally mature exploration of a relationship that once was and clearly had glorious elements, without wanting to go back to that relationship. The lyrics themselves are so specific and yet not tethered down to any specific person, leaving the imagination to do it's wonders.

The song is a nostalgic reflection of a relationship where several things were involved: a golf swing, a trampoline, a crystal ball, red wine and ginger ale. "Little Freak" does an excellent job at creating vivid images and expressing pain and regret, but not in an obvious way. It does so in a way that almost says: "It hurts to miss you, but it was beautiful and I'm glad it happened." Harry doesn't want the relationship back and he also doesn't resent them for finding happiness outside of their relationship- he just thinks about them sometimes.

Perhaps the biggest punch in the gut is in the third verse where Harry sings: "I disrespected you, Jumped in feet first, then I landed too hard/A broken ankle, karma rules/You never saw my birthmark." Through this we get the biggest instance of Harry's regret present in the song towards his partner by the implication that he feels the breakdown of the relationship was his fault that ultimately ended up hurting him. But also, the last line expresses regret in things perhaps ending too soon – before his lover was able to get close enough to see his birthmark. This line could also mean the relationship ended before Harry was able to show his lover the truest parts of himself, and he regrets it.

MATILDA

You were riding your bike to the sound of it's no big deal
And you're trying to lift off the ground on those old two wheels
Nothing 'bout the way you were treated ever seemed especially
alarming 'til now
So you tie up your hair and you smile like it's no big deal
You can let it go
You can throw a party full of everyone you know
And not invite your family 'cause they never showed you love
You don't have to be sorry for leaving and growing up, mmh
Matilda, you talk of the pain like it's all alright
But I know that you feel like a piece of you is dead inside
You showed me a power that is strong enough to bring sun to the
darkest days
It's none of my business but it's been on my mind
You can let it go
You can throw a party full of everyone you know
And not invite your family 'cause they never showed you love
You don't have to be sorry for leaving and growing up
You can see the world
Following the seasons
Anywhere you go
You don't need a reason 'cause they never showed you love
You don't have to be sorry for doing it on your own
You're just in time make your tea and your toast
A friend all you post is that you're close, oh
You don't have to go
You don't have to go home
Oh, there's a long way to go
I don't believe that time will change your mind
In other words
I know they won't you hurt anymore as long as you can let them go
You can let it go
You can throw a party full of everyone you know
You can start a family who will always show you love
You don't have to be sorry for doing it on your own
You can let it go
You can throw a party full of everyone you know
You can start a family who will always show you love
You don't have to be sorry, no

MATILDA

Matilda...where to start??? Well let's first look at what Harry has to say himself:

"I had an experience with someone where, in getting to know them better, they revealed some stuff to me that was very much like, 'Oh, that's not normal, like I think you should maybe get some help or something.' This song was inspired by that experience and person, who I kind of disguised as Matilda from the Roald Dahl book. I played it to a couple of friends and all of them cried. So I was like, 'Okay, I think this is something to pay attention to.' It's a weird one, because with something like this, it's like, 'I want to give you something, I want to support you in some way, but it's not necessarily my place to make it about me because it's not my experience.' Sometimes it's just about listening. I hope that's what I did here. If nothing else, it just says, 'I was listening to you.'"

In the song, Harry somberly sings to somebody whose family did not treat her well, someone who has grown accustomed to a toxic relationship with her family, who 'never showed her love'. He takes inspiration from the Roald Dahl book Matilda, about a girl with telekinesis who was mistreated by her principal and parents. Though Roald Dahl's character Matilda is gendered as female, Styles purposefully does not assign a label to the person he sings to. The song asserts a common theme in the album that home is not a place, but a state of mind. Styles does this by showing how Matilda's house was not a home to her. The way he perceives it, Matilda has the whole world in front of her. So instead of going back to her familial foundation and perpetually reliving the sorrow, the way he sees it is that she shouldn't associate with those people.

CINEMA

You got, you got the cinema
It's you
And I'm not gettin' over it
Darlin', is it cool
If I'm stubborn when it comes to this?
I guess we're in time
If you're getting yourself wet for me
I guess you're all mine
You're sleeping in this bed with me
I just think you're cool
I dig your cinema
Do you think I'm cool too?
Or am I too into you?
Tell me what you want and you got it, love
I want all of you, gimme all you got
That's cinema
That's cinema, uh-huh
It's you
Don't know why, but it feels so right to me
Something in the way you move
I like it when you dance for me (I just think it's-)
You all the time (time, time)
In doses at night (night, night)
No roof on the drive
Dust off the high
And go to sleep (go to sleep, go to sleep)
I just think you're cool
I dig your cinema
Do you think I'm cool, too?
Or am I too into you?
I just think you're cool (co-cool)
I dig your cinema (cinema)
Do you think I'm cool, too?
Or am I (cinema) too into you?
Cinema
You got, you got
I bring the pop, you pop
You got, you got
I bring the pop
You got, you got the cinema
I bring the pop to the cinema, you pop
You got, you got the cinema
You got, you got the cinema
I bring the pop to the cinema
You pop when we get intimate
You got, you got the cinema
You got, you got (cinema) the cinema
I bring the pop to the cinema
You pop when we get intimate (baby, you're cinema)
You got, you got the cinema
You got, you got the cinema
I bring the pop to the cinema
You pop when we get intimate (baby, you're cinema)
You got, you got the cinema
You got, you got the cinema
I bring the pop to the cinema
You pop when we get intimate (baby, you're cinema)
You got, you got the cinema
You got, you got the cinema (cinema)
I bring the pop to the cinema
You pop when we get intimate

CINEMA

The song is about a person whom Harry is infatuated with. They carry certain magic about them, which Harry refers to as a 'cinema.' It sees Styles singing about the early, uncertain phase of a relationship. He worries he isn't cool enough for the person he is with and is nervous that he might come on too strong. The song's emotional arc finds Styles being a confident man at the song's ending, basking in the happiness of mutual affection (and great s*x) brings him.

The song speaks of wanting to spend time just being in each other's presence and letting their feelings grow naturally. Through the lyrics, he wants to know if his feelings are reciprocated, asking him if the person thinks he is cool as well. The chorus emphasizes this feeling with the lyrics "Do you think I'm cool, too?" He compares the feeling he has to being in a movie, describing the person and their presence as "cinema". In the end, it's a love song about a desire for both parties to share the same level of adoration the narrator has for the other person.

A lot of speculation has built around "Cinema" that the song is about Harry Style's ex-partner and Hollywood actress Olivia Wilde. The two met back in 2020 when Styles started working on Wilde's film 'Don't Worry Darling' .When Harry sings "I dig your cinema," he could be referring to the literal movies Olivia Wilde has acted in as well as the cinematic aura she carries which enchants Harry.

DAYDREAMING

Ooh-ooh
Ooh
Livin' in a daydream
She said, "Love me like you paid me"
You know I'll be gone for so long
So give me all of your love, give me something to dream about
Ooh-ooh
Stay until the morning
'Cause, baby, loving you's the real thing
It just feels right
When you give me all of your love, give me something to dream about
(All of your love, give me something to dream about)
So give me all of your love, give me something to dream about
Ooh-ooh
Livin' in a daydream
Livin' in a daydream
Livin' in a daydream
Give me all of your love, give me something to dream about
Livin' in a daydream
Livin' in a daydream (it's alright)
Livin' in a daydream
Give me all of your love
Give me something to dream about (give me all of your love, ooh-ooh)
Give me all of your love
Give me something to dream about (ooh-ooh, it's alright, ooh-ooh)
Give me all of your love
Give me something to dream about (ow)

DAYDREAMING

"Daydreaming" by Harry Styles is a dreamy track that captures the feeling of being lovesick and yearning for something more. Harry talks about living in a daydream, while he asks the person he loves to love him like they paid them. This phrase expresses his wish for a meaningful connection, rather than one that was purchased. Furthermore, it could be a reference to his song 'Fine Line' where he had to buy her love and emotions.

The chorus stresses the idea of living in a daydream, and it becomes a mantra for both the narrator and the listener to let go and live in the moment. Despite the heavy emotions expressed throughout the song, the chorus paints a light and airy picture of acceptance in being able to just live in a daydream.
Overall, the song talks about the beauty of being in a state of longing, and it encourages the listener to just live in the moment and embrace the feelings of being in love.

It is one of the more-straightforward love songs found on the album of 2022. When someone puts forth that they feel like they're "living in a daydream" as the result of a romantic relationship, it's an allegory that we can all easily understand and relate to. The fun and upbeat nature of the song creates a sense of adventure and freedom and is perfect for those who look to live a care-free life, like that of a daydream.

KEEP DRIVING

Black and white film camera
Yellow sunglasses
Ashtray, swimming pool
Hot wax, jump off the roof
A small concern with how the engine sounds
We held darkness in withheld clouds
I would ask, "Should we just keep driving?"
Maple syrup, coffee
Pancakes for two
Hash brown, egg yolk
I will always love you
A small concern with how the engine sounds
We held darkness in withheld clouds
I would ask, "Should we just keep driving?"
Should we just keep driving?
Passports in footwells
Kiss her and don't tells
Wine glass, puff pass, tea with cyborgs
Riot America, science and edibles
Life hacks going viral in the bathroom
Cocaine, side boob
Choke her with a sea view
Toothache, bad move
Just act normal
Moka pot Monday, it's all good
Hey, you
Should we just keep driving?
Should we just keep driving?
Ooh-ooh, ooh
Should we just keep driving?

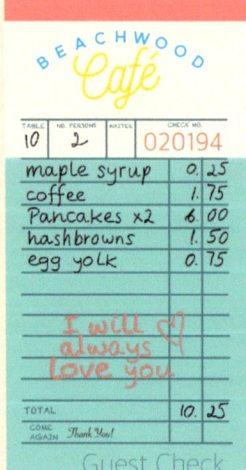

BEACHWOOD
Café

TABLE	NO. PERSONS	WAITER	CHECK NO.
10	2		020194

maple syrup		0.	25
coffee		1.	75
Pancakes x2		6.	00
hashbrowns		1.	50
egg yolk		0.	75
I will ♥ always love you			
TOTAL		10.	25

COME AGAIN   Thank You!

Guest Check

KEEP DRIVING

"Keep Driving", the tenth song on the album, is a loving observation about a long-term relationship worth holding onto despite the presence of troubling truths and general chaos. It is a song about ignoring everything else in the world and when everything is going downhill, you and your loved one just "keep driving". In a metaphorical sense, the phrase "keep driving" refers to trying to move past all the crazy stuff in the world and going about your day despite everything else falling to pieces. There could be some red flags that he has noticed in the relationship but he is choosing to ignore those and focus on their future.

Additionally, the song could be a reference to the COVID pandemic lockdowns. It could be talking about how difficult it was to keep going through the darkness that was lockdown. At the start, Harry lists items ie. a camera and sunglasses, now you may be wondering what does this have to do with the pandemic? Harry lists things that you can find commonly within a house that he was interacting with, whilst he was living with his friends during heavy lockdown. He's using these to set the scene of the song whilst exploring a deeper meaning. It expresses the difficulties to "Keep Driving" and maintain hope during a period of uncertainty and isolation, a feeling that many of us shared. However, in typical Harry fashion, he emphasises the importance of staying positive in these times. A key lyric to this idea is "Tea with cyborgs": this could be a reference to the use of technology to stay in touch with loved ones

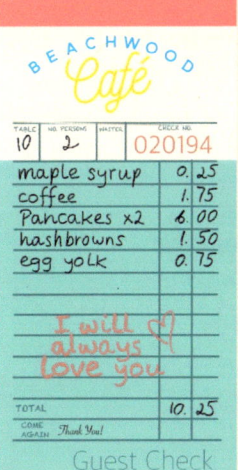

SATELLITE

You got a new life
Am I bothering you?
Do you wanna talk?
We share the last line
Then we drink the wall
'Til we wanna talk
I go 'round and 'round
Satellite
Spinning out, waiting for ya to pull me in
I can see you're lonely down there
Don't you know that I am right here?
Spinning out, waiting for ya to pull me in
I can see you're lonely down there
Don't you know that I am right here?
Spinning out, waiting for ya
I'm in an L.A. mood
I don't wanna talk to you
She said, "Give me a day or two"
I go 'round and 'round
Satellite
Spinning out, waiting for ya to pull me in
I can see you're lonely down there
Don't you know that I am right here?
Spinning out, waiting for you to pull me in
I can see you're lonely down there
Don't you know that I am right here?
Right here, right here
Spinning out, waiting for ya
I'm here, right here
Wishing I could be there for ya
Be there for ya
Be there for ya, for ya
(For ya)
(Be there for ya)
Spinning out, waiting for ya to pull me in (spinning out, waiting)
I can see you're lonely down there
Don't you know that I am right here?
Spinning out waiting for ya (for ya, for ya) to pull me in (for ya)
I can see you're lonely down there
Don't you know that I am right here?
Spinning out, waiting for ya (for ya, for ya) to pull me in (for ya)
I can see you're lonely down there
Don't you know that I am right here?

SATELLITE

"Satellite" is anchored around this notion of aimlessly going around and around in circles — ya know, kind of like a satellite. Although an upbeat tune, the lyrics convey the feeling of being lost and broken-hearted. In the first verse, Harry sings, "You got a new life / Am I bothering you? / Do you wanna talk?," which suggests a break-up or failed relationship.

Throughout the song, there's a clear disconnect between Harry and the subject, who's just referred to as "she." Harry sings about "spinning out" and seemingly wanting to be needed and loved by this person, but being distanced from them. The song is about wanting to get closer to someone who seems to be holding back and putting themself at a distance. The refrain of "spinning out, waiting for you to pull me in" illustrates an eagerness to be close and a desire to be the one to reach out. The imagery of the satellite spinning around captures the idea of trying to come closer but constantly missing the connection, while also suggesting a longing for something greater where the two people could transcend their physical distance and bridge the gaps between them. The song speaks to the emotions of being stuck in a place of separation and longing for connection and closeness. It could be about the ups and downs of relationships, the uncontrollable feeling of falling in and out of love, the messiness of break-ups, and the journey of finding oneself. Considering he was still in a relationship with Olivia Wilde at the time, it is possible this song is inspired by a past relationship.

BOYFRIENDS

Boyfriends
They think you're so easy
They take you for granted
They don't know they're just misunderstanding you
You, you're back at it again
Weakened
When you get deep in
He starts secretly drinking
It gets hard to know what he's thinking
You love a fool who knows just how to get under your skin
You, you, you still open the door

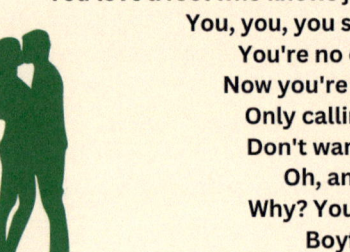

You're no closer to him
Now you're halfway home
Only calling you when
Don't wanna be alone
Oh, and you go
Why? You don't know
Boyfriends
Are they just pretending?
They don't tell you where it's heading
And you know the game's never ending
You, you lay with him as you stay in the daydream
You feel a fool
You're back at it again
Ooh

To Boyfriends Everywhere
Fuck you

'To boyfriends everywhere...f*ck you'- wise words from Harry, as always. The song reveals the way many boyfriends tend to mistreat their partners by mediating on a troubled relationship between two people. He very astutely points out that being taken for granted isn't something that's always obvious and immediate, but your instincts always tell you when something isn't quite right. He suggests that being with someone for a long time 'weakens' you because you're more attached to you and they know just how to get under your skin. The individual is stuck in a loop, where they get mistreated, but let their boyfriend back into their life, remaining oblivious to the situation. He makes a point to show that this will have consequences.

The song is inspired by a combination of his own experiences, seeing people settle for less than they deserve, and his observations of others in a similar situation. In an interview with Zane Lowe of Apple Music, Harry Styles explained that "Boyfriends" was inspired by watching her sister's dating life as well as his own: *"I think the good part of ["Boyfriends"] is that it is everything. It's both acknowledging my own behavior. It's looking at behavior that I've witnessed. I grew up with a sister, so it's watching her date people and watching friends date people, and people don't treat each other very nicely sometimes. It was one of those really quick, just say what you think of boyfriends."*

LOVE OF MY LIFE

Baby, you were the love of my life, woah
Maybe you don't know what's lost 'til you find it
Take a walk on Sunday through the afternoon
We can always find somethin' for us to do
We don't really like what's on the news, but it's on all the time
I take you with me every time I go away
In a hotel, usin' someone else's name
I remember back at Jonny's place, it's not the same anymore
Baby, you were the love of my life, woah
Maybe you don't know what's lost 'til you find it
It's not what I wanted, to leave you behind
Don't know where you'll land when you fly
But, baby, you were the love of my life
It's unfortunate, ooh
Just coordinates, ooh
I don't know you half as well as all my friends
I won't pretend that I've been doin' everything I can
To get to know your creases and your ends
Are they the same?
Baby, you were the love of my life, woah
Maybe you don't know what's lost 'til you find it
It's not what I wanted, to leave you behind
Don't know where you'll land when you fly
But, baby, you were the love of my life

LOVE OF MY LIFE

Finally, his last song is certainly one to finish on. In the song, Harry talks about realizing a person's true value when they are already gone from his life—a tale as old as time. It is an admission of defeat and loss by Harry Styles. Most of us don't realize the value of what we have until we lose them. The same goes for relationships of all kinds—parents, siblings, friends, and partners. The truth settles in later on and later is just too late. The first verse of Harry Styles' "Love of My Life" acts like a reminiscing of what he and his ex-partner used to do such as taking strolls on Sunday afternoon and watching the news. Even when they have to part ways, he has something to remember his partner by that he takes with him everywhere. After a breakup, we usually tend to relive memories whenever one passes by places visited together with an ex. Harry is no different in this sense, as he finds himself going through the memories associated to such places, bringing him much sadness.

However although "Love Of My Life" sure sounds like a song of longing for a former romantic partner that slipped away, but the emotional ballad isn't about a person, it's about Harry Styles' country of birth: "I've always wanted to write a song about like home and loving England and all that kind of stuff," he told Apple Music. "And it's always kinda hard to do without being like 'went to the chippy and I did this thing'". He goes on to reflect on the good times he had living in England, such as Sunday walks. With production full of warm chords and synths, the track's stripped energy can be felt with each verse and it is clear his hometown holds a special place in his heart. Toward the end of the track, Styles admits that even though his time with the country was limited, it was still "the love of his life."

Made in United States
Troutdale, OR
07/25/2023

11539255R10019